W9-BCI-107

MPIONSHIP:

2016

WITHDRAWN

ALL-TIME LEADING SCORER:

**THE NBA:
A HISTORY
OF HOOPS**

CLEVELAND
CAVALIERS

LeBRON JAMES (2003–10, 2014–PRESENT):

20,868 POINTS

(AS OF APRIL 13, 2017)

THE NBA: A HISTORY OF HOOPS

CLEVELAND CAVALIERS

BY JIM WHITING

CREATIVE EDUCATION CREATIVE PAPERBACKS

Published by Creative Education
and Creative Paperbacks

P.O. Box 227, Mankato, Minnesota 56002

Creative Education and Creative Paperbacks
are imprints of The Creative Company

www.thecreativecompany.us

Design and production by Blue Design
Printed in the United States of America

Photographs by Corbis (Bettmann), Getty Images
(Steve Babineau/NBA, Mark Blinch/Getty Images
Sport, Nathaniel S. Butler/NBA, Focus on Sport/
Getty Images Sport, Jesse D. Garrabrant/NBAE,
Jeff Goode/Toronto Star, David Liam Kyle/NBA,
Ronald Martinez/Getty Images Sport, Manny
Millan/Sports Illustrated, Greg Nelson/Sports
Illustrated, Nivek Neslo, Dick Raphael/NBA, Rogers
Photo Archive/Getty Images Sport, Gregory
Shamus/Getty Images Sport, Carl Skalak/Sports
Illustrated, Carl Skalak/Sports Illustrated Classic,
Tom Szczerbowski/Getty Images Sport, Tony
Tomsic/Sports Illustrated), Newscom (Mitchell
Layton/MCT, Ting Shen/Xinhua/Photoshot)

Library of Congress Cataloging-in-Publication Data

Names: Whiting, Jim, 1943- author.

Title: Cleveland Cavaliers / Jim Whiting.

Series: The NBA: A History of Hoops.

Includes bibliographical references and index.

Summary: This high-interest title summarizes the
history of the Cleveland Cavaliers professional
basketball team, highlighting memorable events
and noteworthy players such as LeBron James.

Identifiers: LCCN 2016046225 / ISBN 978-1-60818-
840-6 (hardcover) / ISBN 978-1-62832-443-3
(pbk) / ISBN 978-1-56660-888-6 (eBook)

Subjects: LCSH: 1. Cleveland Cavaliers
(Basketball team)—History—Juvenile
literature. 2. Cleveland Cavaliers (Basketball
team)—Biography—Juvenile literature.

Classification: LCC GV885.52.C57 W55 2017 /
DDC 796.323/640977132—dc23

CCSS: RI.4.1, 2, 3, 4; RI.5.1, 2, 4; RI.6.1, 2,
3; RF.4.3, 4; RF.5.3, 4; RH. 6-8. 4, 5, 7

First Edition HC 9 8 7 6 5 4 3 2 1
First Edition PBK 9 8 7 6 5 4 3 2 1

A hub of transportation, **CLEVELAND** sits where the Cuyahoga River flows into Lake Erie.

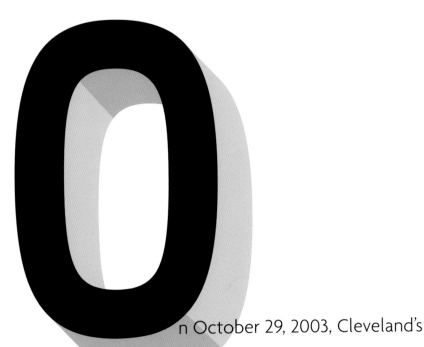

CLEVELAND JOINS THE NBA

On October 29, 2003, Cleveland's Gund Arena shook with anticipation. LeBron James was about to make his National Basketball Association (NBA) debut with the Cleveland Cavaliers. James was

The Cavaliers slowly improved until they reached the playoffs in 1975–76.

a swashbuckling cavalier. He looked like one of the Three Musketeers. He wore a floppy hat, cape, and high boots and carried a sword.

There wasn't much action in the first season. The team consisted of veterans other teams didn't want and a handful of untested rookies. Coach Bill Fitch was realistic about the team's chances. "Remember, my name is Fitch, not Houdini," he said. The Cavs lost their first 15 games. They edged fellow expansion team Portland by two points for their first victory. Then the Cavs dropped another 12 in a row. They finished 15–67. It was the league's worst record.

TASTING SUCCESS AND FAILURE

16

C leveland had the first pick in the 1971 NBA Draft. It took 6-foot-4 shooting guard Austin Carr. He became the face of the team.

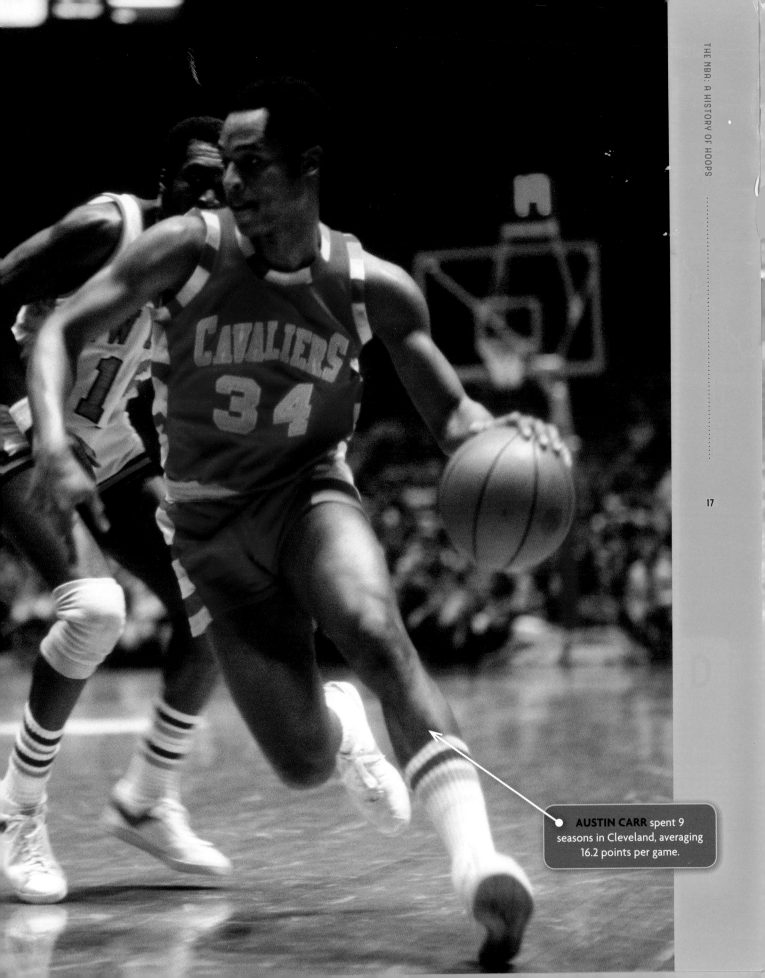

AUSTIN CARR spent 9 seasons in Cleveland, averaging 16.2 points per game.

literally shaking. That season is when basketball in Cleveland was born."
Unfortunately, Chones broke his foot in practice before the next round.
Cleveland played hard against the Boston Celtics. But they lost the
series, four games to two.

itch guided the Cavs to 43–39 records the following two
seasons, but there were no more miracles. The Cavs were bounced in the
first round of the playoffs both times. They stumbled to a 30–52 mark
in 1978–79. Fitch quit. After another losing record, Mileti sold the team
to Ted Stepien. The next three years were the low point of Cavaliers
history. Stepien proved to be one of the worst owners in NBA history.
Guard World B. Free was one of the few bright spots. He joined the team
in 1982. He soon became the leading scorer. "World sincerely believes
every shot he takes will go in," said fellow guard John Bagley. "A lot of
times, he's right."

LEGENDS OF THE HARDWOOD

WORST NBA OWNER?

TED STEPIEN, OWNER, 1980–83

Owner Ted Stepien was a poor judge of talent. He traded high draft choices for marginal veterans. He tried to schedule "home games" in other states. He even made racist comments. Fans called the team the Cleveland Cadavers because they lost so many games. The *New York Times* said the Cavs were "the worst club and most poorly run franchise in professional basketball." When Stepien sold the team, the NBA realized his ownership had been a disaster. The league granted the Cavaliers extra first-round draft picks for four years. Now, the "Stepien Rule" forbids a team from trading its top draft choice two years in a row.

REPAIRING THE DAMAGE

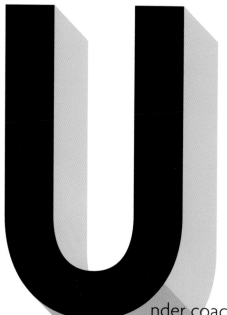

nder coach Lenny Wilkens, the Cavs finally had a winning season again in 1987–88, going 42–40. They had drafted 7-foot center Brad Daugherty and explosive guard Ron Harper the previous

Seven-foot center **BRAD DAUGHERTY** led Cleveland to the playoffs six times.

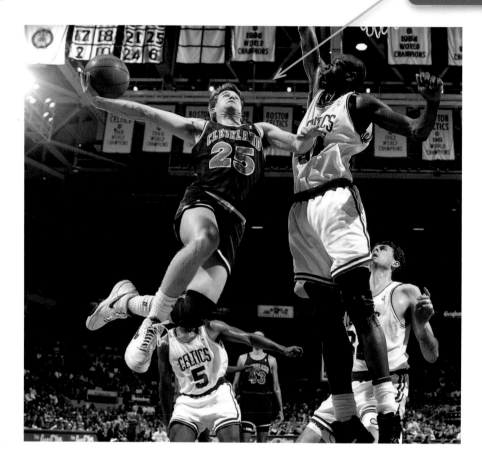

A quick release and perfect form made **MARK PRICE** one of the NBA's top shooters.

year. They added sharpshooting point guard Mark Price and long-limbed power forward Larry Nance. But Cleveland lost to Chicago in the first round of the playoffs. Everything meshed the following year. The Cavs went 57–25. It was their best record. Once again, they couldn't get past Chicago in the playoffs. Injuries and bad trades plagued the Cavs the next two seasons. They bounced back in 1991–92, winning 57 games. But they lost to the Bulls in the Eastern Conference finals, four games to two. When the Bulls bounced the Cavs from the playoffs yet again in 1992–93, Wilkens was done. "It's been a great seven years with the Cavaliers," he said. "However, I think it's time to move on." Defensive-

LEGENDS OF THE HARDWOOD

FROM HERO TO GOAT

GAME 5, EASTERN CONFERENCE PLAYOFFS, CLEVELAND VS. CHICAGO, MAY 7, 1989

Cleveland's Craig Ehlo had scored Cleveland's last eight points. His final basket gave the Cavs a 100–99 lead. Seconds remained. The Bulls' Michael Jordan went up for a jump shot. He suspended himself in midair long enough for Ehlo to sail past him. With one second left, he released the ball. It went in. Chicago won 101–100. The ESPN TV network called it the best play of Jordan's career. "If I hadn't been out of position I could have stopped that shot," Ehlo said later. "I had a hand in his face but only for a split second."

TRAVELING COURT

In 1997, tiny Grace Christian School in Staunton, Virginia, wanted its own basketball court. The school learned that the court and baskets of Richfield Coliseum (pictured) were available. A local contractor donated an empty warehouse. It would be the school's gym. A trucking company donated two big rigs to bring the floor to Virginia. The Cavs did their part. Another school offered more money. The Cavs stood by the original deal. Today the floor still displays the Cavs logo. It reminds the school's athletes of its heritage. "All the greats played on this floor," said girls' basketball coach Randall McNair.

minded Mike Fratello replaced him. "I'd rather win ugly than lose pretty," said the new coach. Ugly or not, the team kept winning for several more seasons. But Cleveland still made early playoff exits.

The Cavs missed out on a golden opportunity in the 1996 NBA Draft. They chose 6-foot-10 center Vitaly Potapenko. Nicknamed the "Ukraine Train," he lasted less than three seasons and averaged just 7 points a game. Cleveland fans watched the three selections right after Potapenko go on to superstardom. They were Kobe Bryant, Peja Stojaković, and Steve Nash. Both Bryant and Nash were named Most Valuable Player (MVP). Stojaković became an All-Star. A three-way trade brought power forward Shawn Kemp to Cleveland in 1997. He was a starter in the 1998 All-Star Game. The following year, he averaged more than 20 points a game. Soon, Fratello moved on. Without him, the team endured several losing seasons. Injuries, constant coaching changes, and roster turnover hounded the team. The Cavs of the early 2000s often appeared to be playing street ball. They sported flashy style but lacked teamwork.

KING JAMES REIGNS

Cleveland bottomed out in 2002–03 with a 17–65 record. It was the team's worst mark in 21 years. The dismal showing gave the Cavs the first pick in the 2003 NBA Draft. There was no question about whom they would choose: LeBron James. James

33

Averaging 30 points per game in 2007–08, LEBRON JAMES topped the league in scoring.

As of 2016, **JAMES** had earned All-Star status eight times while with the Cavs.

34

had played high school ball in nearby Akron. He led his team to three state championships. He was on the cover of *Sports Illustrated*. Twice he was named Gatorade National Player of the Year.

James lived up to the hype. He scored 25 points in his first game. "I thought he was going to be good, but not nearly as good as he was," said coach Paul Silas. "It was unbelievable." Later that season, he became the youngest player in NBA history to score at least 40 points in a game. He was just the third rookie to average at least 20 points, 5 rebounds, and 5 assists. Not surprisingly, he was selected Rookie of the Year. He helped Cleveland win 35 games, doubling its record from the year before. In the previous season, average attendance was 11,497. It rose to 18,288 in James's first season. James was even better in 2004–05. He averaged 27.2 points, 7.4 rebounds, 7.2 assists, and 2.2 steals per game. He became the youngest player named to the All-NBA team. Cleveland narrowly missed the playoffs, finishing 42–40.

In Cleveland from 2008 to 2010, **MO WILLIAMS** returned for the title-winning season.

> "WE BELIEVE IT WILL BE A GOLDEN ERA OF BASKETBALL FOR THE FANS AND COMMUNITY OF THIS HARDWORKING AND WELL-DESERVING TOWN."

Quicken Loans founder Dan Gilbert bought the team before the 2005–06 season. "We believe it will be a golden era of basketball for the fans and community of this hardworking and well-deserving town," he said. That "golden era" got off to a good start. The Cavs won 50 games. The first round of the playoffs echoed the Miracle of Richfield. Cleveland beat the Washington Wizards by a point in two overtime games to win the series 4–2. But it lost to Detroit in the next round. In 2006–07, the Cavs played in the NBA Finals for the first time. But San Antonio was too tough. The Spurs swept the series. Cleveland advanced to the conference semifinals the following year. Boston bounced them out. James had a sensational season in 2008–09. He averaged 28.4 points, 7.6 rebounds, and 7.2 assists per game. He was also runner-up for Defensive Player of the Year. He earned his first MVP award. Plus, he led the team to a franchise-record 66 wins. Another key to success was point guard Mo Williams. The Cavs swept both Detroit and Atlanta in the playoffs. But Cleveland lost the Eastern Conference finals to Orlando. James repeated as MVP the following year. But when the Cavs lost in the conference semifinals, James was booed.

JAMES fired up Cleveland fans with his ritualistic pregame "chalk toss."

BREAKING—AND MENDING—A CITY'S HEART

n 2010, James became a free agent. That meant he could sign with any team. He announced his choice in a TV show called *The Decision*. The program

40

LeBRON JAMES: NFL STAR?

LeBRON JAMES, FORWARD, 6-FOOT-8, 2003–10, 2014–PRESENT

LeBron James played wide receiver for his high school football team for two years. Ohio State and Notre Dame wanted him to play football for them. Some people even think he could play in the National Football League (NFL). "He's a 6-foot-8, 250-pound freak of stature," wrote ESPN's Tim Graham. "He would tower above NFL defensive backs and other receivers." Players such as Green Bay safety Mark Murphy agreed. "I felt like that was one kid that could have gone from high school to the NFL," he said. James even made a brief appearance in the *Madden NFL 12* video game.

raised $6 million for charity. But there was no charity for Cleveland fans. James said he was joining the Miami Heat. Moments later, he became one of the most disliked athletes in the country. Cleveland exploded. Gilbert published an open letter criticizing James. Fans burned his jersey.

41

ithout James, the Cavs scraped together just 19 wins in the 2010–11 season. Cleveland traded Williams to the Los Angeles Clippers for guard Baron Davis. Davis played the final 15 games of the season before being released. However, the Cavs struck gold in the NBA Draft for the second time in less than a decade. The Williams trade gave them the top overall pick. With it, Cleveland chose point guard Kyrie Irving. Irving became an instant sensation. He averaged 18.5 points and 5.4 assists per game. He was named Rookie of the Year. Despite his accomplishments, Cleveland still struggled. The team won just 21 games in the strike-shortened

2011–12 season, then 24 and 33 the following two seasons.

Everything changed on July 11, 2014. Two weeks earlier, LeBron James once again had become a free agent. Where would he go this time? An article in *Sports Illustrated* provided the answer. "When I left Cleveland, I was on a mission," James said. "I was seeking championships, and we won two. But Miami already knew that feeling. Our city [Cleveland] hasn't had that feeling in a long, long, long time. My goal is still to win as many titles as possible, no question. But what's most important for me is bringing one trophy back to Northeast Ohio." Fans immediately forgave him for leaving four years earlier. As a bonus, James persuaded big man Kevin Love to join him in Cleveland. With Irving, the team could now boast a Big Three. Swingman Tristan Thompson added strength from the bench. Cleveland roared to a 53–29 record in the regular season. The Cavs swept both Boston and Atlanta in the playoffs. They blasted into the 2015 NBA Finals. But the Golden State Warriors were just too tough. The Warriors won the series four games to two.

Mo Williams returned to the Cavs at the start of the 2015–16 season. In a way, that meant Cleveland got Irving … for free. With 57 wins, the Cavs charged into the playoffs. Easy series wins over Detroit, Atlanta, and Toronto propelled them into the NBA Finals. "I came back for a reason," James said after the Cavs knocked off the Warriors. "I came back to bring a championship to our city. I knew what I was capable of doing."

TRISTAN THOMPSON provided solid defense and rebounding, especially in James's absence.

Big man **KEVIN LOVE** helped the Cavs defeat the Warriors in the 2016 NBA Finals.

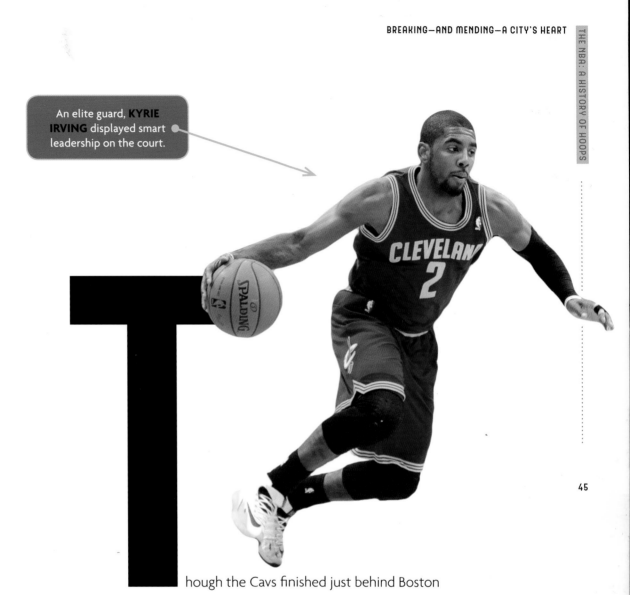

An elite guard, **KYRIE IRVING** displayed smart leadership on the court.

45

Though the Cavs finished just behind Boston in the Eastern Conference in 2016–17, they made it through the first three rounds of the playoffs with only one loss. They faced Golden State for the third year in a row in the Finals. James became the first player in NBA history to average a triple-double in the Finals. He also surpassed Michael Jordan to become the all-time playoffs scoring leader. But there would be no miracle finish for Cleveland that year. The Cavs won just one game.

Cleveland fans loyally supported the Cavs through all their ups and downs. They rejoiced when native son LeBron James led the team to its first-ever NBA title. They look forward to more championship banners hanging inside Quicken Loans Arena very soon.

SELECTED BIBLIOGRAPHY

Ballard, Chris. *The Art of a Beautiful Game: The Thinking Fan's Tour of the NBA*. New York: Simon & Schuster, 2010.

Hubbard, Jan, ed. *The Official NBA Basketball Encyclopedia*. 3rd edition. New York: Doubleday, 2000.

McKee, Vincent. *The Cleveland Cavaliers: A History of the Wine and Gold*. Charleston, S.C.: Arcadia, 2014.

NBA.com. "Cleveland Cavaliers." http://www.nba.com /cavaliers/.

Simmons, Bill. *The Book of Basketball: The NBA According to the Sports Guy*. New York: Ballantine, 2009.

Sports Illustrated. *Sports Illustrated Basketball's Greatest*. New York: Sports Illustrated, 2014.

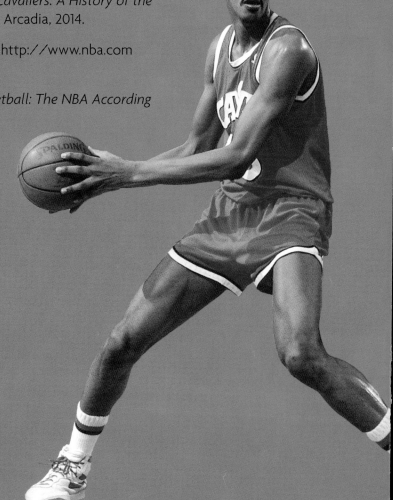